My RSVP

to Accept God's Invitation to Enjoy the Pleasure of His Company

PRAYER GUIDE

Judy Warpole

WestBow
PRESS
A DIVISION OF THOMAS NELSON

WestBow Press books may be ordered through booksellers or by contacting:

WestBow Press
A Division of Thomas Nelson
1663 Liberty Drive
Bloomington, IN 47403
www.westbowpress.com
1-(866) 928-1240

Because of the dynamic nature of the Internet, any web addresses or links contained in this book may have changed since publication and may no longer be valid. The views expressed in this work are solely those of the author and do not necessarily reflect the views of the publisher, and the publisher hereby disclaims any responsibility for them.

Any people depicted in stock imagery provided by Thinkstock are models, and such images are being used for illustrative purposes only.

Certain stock imagery © Thinkstock.

ISBN: 978-1-4908-0432-3 (sc)

Library of Congress Control Number: 2013914231

Printed in the United States of America.

WestBow Press rev. date: 08/20/2013

"Pray in the Spirit

ON ALL OCCASIONS

with all kinds of prayers and requests.

With this in mind,

be alert and always keep on praying...."

Ephesians 6:18 NIV

Contents

Thoughts Before Praying

When the words of Jesus, "Come with me by yourselves to a quiet place and get some rest" (Mark 6:31 NIV), describe the longing within you to spend time with God, take this *My RSVP* prayer guide in hand. The words within will guide you as you draw near to God.

Each instruction plus every scripture and prayer will open the way to a more intimate communication with God. The inspired words of scripture will express what has always been, and is now, in the eternal mind and heart of Our Father. The prayers are your response to Him. As you get into the flow, you will sense that you are participating in a two-way spiritual conversation with God Himself.

As you repeat in prayer what you have read in the words of God, you will be confessing to Him that you hear Him and that you desire to live by every word that comes from His mouth (Matthew 4:4).

"When do I use this prayer guide," you ask. *My RSVP* chapters 1 through 13 can be used in many ways and at different times.

- ➤ All at one time when you have an hour or two to spend in the pleasure of His company
- ➤ A section each day during your devotional and prayer time
- ➤ A particular section as a personal need arises
- ➤ Over and over again as needed

PRAY IN THE BEAUTY OF GOD'S CREATION:

Occasionally you will be able to arrange your time so you can take your Bible and *My RSVP* to a favorite spot surrounded by the beauty of nature, just as Jesus frequently did when He went into the garden to pray (Luke 22:37, 39). These will be the special times when you can delight yourself in the pleasure of His company for as long as you desire.

EARLY IN THE MORNING:

Even though you might desire to spend an hour or more each day in the pleasure of Our Father's company, other demands and responsibilities may not always afford you this privilege. However, you can train yourself to awaken in the morning thinking about eternity. Before opening your eyes, greet Our Father in heaven—praising Him for the holiness of His name.

As your day progresses, if worrisome, troubling thoughts rush in, give yourself enough time to express to Our Father what distresses you. Talk it through until your anxious thoughts are replaced with His precious peace that transcends all understanding (Philippians 4:6-7).

PRAY THROUGHOUT THE DAY:

As people who are lost or straying from God, come into your thoughts, pray for His kingdom—His sovereign rule and reign—to come upon them. And when decisions must be made, your sentences of prayer spoken to Him aloud or silently from your mind can request that you do His will in all things as His will is done in heaven.

PRAY AT MEALTIME:

During your meals you may pray and rejoice in thanksgiving because your daily bread is provided so abundantly—both physically and spiritually. When there is little time for a full spiritual meal, a verse here and a verse there can become like snack food for quick strength during those times when your energy levels are low . . . until you can feast fully on His word again.

PRAY ALONG THE WAY:

As your day progresses, you may find yourself reflecting upon your attitudes and actions so that your rapid response is to pray, "Forgive me my sins as I forgive everyone who sins against me. And lead me not into temptation, but deliver me from the evil one."

PRAY AT THE END OF THE DAY:

On those days when you cannot spend an hour or more in the pleasure of His company, but must communicate your prayers along the way throughout the day . . . when you finally come to the end of the day, close your eyes and savor the joy that is yours because He has allowed you another day to share in His kingdom and power and glory. Close your eyes and quietly rejoice because He has called you to enjoy the pleasure of His company forever. Amen.

PRAY AFTER THE END OF THE DAY:

There are times when you say, "This has been one of those days!" Jesus also had "those days"! Busy, pressure-filled, fragmented, disappointing, troublesome, draining days. We are told that during these times in His life, on "one of those days Jesus went out to a mountainside to pray, and spent the night praying to God" (Luke 6:12 NIV).

There will be times when you cannot sleep. Instead of tossing and turning, get up and pray so that you will not fall into temptation (Luke 22:46). Find a quiet place, close the door and pray to Our Father (Matthew 6:6).

Overcoming Enemies of Prayer

THE ENEMY	HOW TO OVERCOME
Interruptions	Pick a set time and place when and where you will least likely be interrupted. Get away by yourself. Silence the interruptions over which you have control. (Matthew 6:6)
Disturbing emotions	Play inspirational music. Breathe deeply several times. Sit quietly before beginning to pray. (Psalm 46:10)
Drowsiness	Sit. Stand. Walk. Speak aloud. (Matthew 26:40-41)
Wandering thoughts	Write down your prayers and thoughts. Pray aloud. (Psalm 5:3; Psalm 66:17-19)
Doubts about your prayers	Read God's words. Claim God's promises. Remind yourself that God loves you. Remind yourself that God has invited you to come to Him boldly and with confidence. (Psalm 138:3; Hebrews 4:16)

How To Use *My RSVP* Prayer Guide

- ➤ Find a quiet place where you will least likely be interrupted.

- ➤ Open to page 1 and pause before beginning.

- ➤ If you want, listen to your favorite inspirational music; turn it off before praying if it distracts your thoughts.

- ➤ Close your eyes.

- ➤ Take several deep breathes.

- ➤ With spiritual eyes, visualize the throne of God.

- ➤ When you are ready, begin to read.

- ➤ Go slowly enough to think about what you read.

- ➤ Go through this guide as far as you want based on the time you have allotted to spend in prayer and meditation.

My RSVP

Each *My RSVP* chapter number corresponds to the same chapter number in *The Pleasure of His Company* if you should want to re-read a particular chapter.

READ AND FOLLOW THE INSTRUCTIONS IN BOLD
CAPITAL LETTERS.

When instructions are MEDITATE:

Slowly and carefully read the scriptures shown. Think about
how the words of God apply to your own life. After reading
each scripture, ask yourself if your life is in harmony with
God's words.

When the instructions are PRAY:

In your own words, pray and communicate to God your
responses to His words . . . or . . .

In an attitude of two-way conversation, read the carefully worded
prayers that use God's own words from the meditation scriptures,
affirming to Him that you desire to live by every word that
comes from His mouth (Matthew 4:4). In this way you apply His
words to yourself personally—not adding to nor taking away
from His will (Deuteronomy 12:32, Revelation 22:18-19).

When you come to _____(underlined blank spaces)_____

Instructions for what to insert into the blank spaces are given.
Do not skip over them; rather, use these opportunities to pray
your own words as appropriate for that particular section of
prayer.

When you come to . . .

_____   _____
_____   _____
_____   _____
_____   _____
_____   _____

Follow the instructions to write names of people you want to remember in your prayers. A word of caution: If someone else were to look through your prayer guide, protect the privacy of those named people as well as your own by not writing too many details—just enough to prompt your memory.

My Response to God's Invitation to Enjoy the Pleasure of His Company

> ## My
> # *RSVP*
>
> It is with sincere appreciation that I accept
> God's Invitation to enjoy
>
> *The Pleasure of His Company*

Dear Heavenly Father, it is with sincere appreciation that I accept Your invitation to enjoy the pleasure of Your company. I am delighted to "come with Jesus to a quiet place and get some rest" (Mark 6:31 ESV). Please help me to "be joyful always; pray continually; give thanks in all circumstances, understanding that this is your will for me in Christ Jesus" (1 Thessalonians 5:17-18 ESV). I thank You for the blessing to be able to close the door and pray to You, Father (Matthew 6:6). I am happy to spend time with You, thinking about Your words, and speaking to You about what is on my heart. "May the words of my mouth and the meditation of my heart be pleasing in your sight, O Lord, my Rock and my Redeemer" (Psalm 19:14 NIV).

My RSVP 1

READ GOD'S INSPIRED WORDS AND MEDITATE ON "THE PATH OF LIFE":

> "You make known to me
> the path of life;
> You fill me with joy in your presence,
> with eternal pleasures at your right hand."
> (Psalm 16:11 NIV)

PRAY SLOWLY AND THOUGHTFULLY:

Almighty God, thank You for showing me—through Your inspired words—the path of life which brings me into Your presence so that I might enjoy eternal pleasures at Your right hand (Psalm 16:11). Thank You for the joy that fills me when I am in Your presence. With renewed commitment I promise:

> I WILL submit to You and be at peace with You.
> I WILL accept instruction from Your mouth.
> I WILL return to You so that whenever I sin I might be restored.
> I WILL remove wickedness from my life.
> I WILL find delight in You.
> I WILL pray, believing You hear me.
> I WILL let Jesus be the light of my life.
> (Job 22:21-23, 26-28 NASB paraphrased)

MEDITATE UPON GOD'S INSPIRED PROMISE:

"Delight yourself in the Lord
and He will give you the desires of your heart."
(Psalm 37:4 NASB)

PRAY TO DESIRE WHAT GOD DESIRES:

Lord, I want You to know that I truly desire to find my delight
in You. I trust You to give me the desires of my heart! I ask You
to help me to make my desires more and more like Your desires.
I want to desire those things that bring You pleasure.

I affirm that I desire...

> ... integrity and loyalty to You
> (1 Chronicles 29:17,18 NIV)
> ... the success of all my plans
> (Psalm 20:4 NIV)
> ... to see many good days
> (Psalm 34:12-14 NIV)
> ... to do Your will, O my God
> (Psalm 40:8 NIV)
> ... to want nothing from this earth besides You
> (Psalm 73:25b ESV)
> ... to fear You so that You will hear me and save me
> (Psalm 145:18-20 ESV)
> ... wisdom and understanding
> (Proverbs 3:18,15 ESV)
> ... righteousness and goodness (Proverbs 11:23)
> ... a good name (Proverbs 22:1 NASB)
> ...Your name to be remembered
> (Isaiah 26:8-9 ESV)

... to do what is right (Romans 7:18 ESV)

... to set my mind on what the Spirit desires
(Romans 8:5b NIV)

... the greater gifts: faith, hope and love
(1 Corinthians 12:31 and 13:13 NASB)

... to finish the work I start so that my 'doing'
will be equal to my 'wanting to do'
(2 Corinthians 8:11 NCV)

... to live honorably in every way (Hebrews13:18 ESV)

... to be with Christ in life and in death
(Philippians 1:21-24 ESV)

Father, I believe Your promise that "the desires of the diligent are fully satisfied" (Proverbs 13:4 NIV). Please increase my desire and resolve to be diligent in prayer.

MEDITATE ON JESUS:

- Jesus whose words are the light on my path
(Psalm 119:105)
- Jesus who is the light of the world
(John 8:12)
- Jesus who is the way, the truth and the life
(John 14:6)

CONTINUE TO PRAY:

Father, I truly believe that Your Son Jesus is the Word of God who became flesh and lived among men (John 1:14). I accept Him as the Son of God, and I accept His words as the light for my path and the lamp for my feet (Psalm 119:105). Jesus *is* the light of the world (John 8:12)! He *is* the light of my life! I believe that in Him I will find all truth (John 14:6) about You, Father.

Again I confirm to You that I desire to accept Your invitation to enjoy eternal pleasures at Your right hand. Thank You for this invitation. Please "send Jesus who is Your light and Your truth to guide me and bring me to the place where You dwell. Together we come to Your altar. You are my joy and my delight" (Psalm 43:3-4 NIV paraphrased)!

As I pray, all my words are spoken, and will continue to be spoken in the name of Jesus (John 16:23-24), my intercessor (Hebrews 7:25). Amen.

WRITE THE NAMES OF PEOPLE WHO ENCOURAGE ME ON "THE PATH OF LIFE":

_____   _____
_____   _____
_____   _____
_____   _____
_____   _____
_____   _____
_____   _____
_____   _____
_____   _____
_____   _____

THANK GOD FOR THESE PEOPLE.

My RSVP 2

MEDITATE UPON BUILDING ACCORDING
TO GOD'S PLAN:

"Why do you call me, 'Lord, Lord,' but do not
do what I say? I will show you what everyone
is like who comes to me and hears my words
and obeys. That person is like a man building a
house who dug deep and laid the foundation on
rock." (Luke 6:46-48 NCV)

"... everyone then who hears these words of mine
and does them will be like a wise man who built
his house on the rock." (Matthew 7:24 ESV)

"For no one can lay any foundation other than
the one already laid, which is Jesus Christ." (1
Corinthians 3:11 NIV)

"The wise woman builds her house, but the
foolish tears it down with her own hands."
(Proverbs 14:1 NASB)

"For every house is built by someone, but the
builder of all things is God…. Christ is faithful
over God's house… and we are his house…."
(Hebrews 3:4, 6 ESV)

CONTINUE TO PRAY IN JESUS' NAME:

Lord, please help me to hear Your words and put them into practice. May my words, my actions and my entire life be built upon the rock solid foundation of Jesus Christ. Help me to build with Your wisdom. Thank You for Christ, Your faithful Son, who watches over all of us who are being built together into Your house.

MEDITATE UPON THE ACTIONS OF JESUS AS HE PREPARED HIS HOUSE TO BECOME A HOUSE OF PRAYER:

- **JESUS CLEANED HIS HOUSE.**

  "Jesus entered the temple area and drove out all who were buying and selling there. He overturned the tables of the money changers and the benches of those selling doves.

- **JESUS DEFINED THE PURPOSE OF HIS HOUSE.**

  "'It is written,' he said to them, 'My house will be called a HOUSE OF PRAYER, but you are making it a den of robbers.'

- **JESUS' HOUSE IS A PLACE OF HEALING.**

  "The blind and the lame came to him at the temple, and he healed them.

- **JESUS' HOUSE IS FILLED WITH PRAISE.**

  "But when the chief priests and the teachers of
  the law saw the wonderful things he did and the
  children shouting in the temple area, 'Hosanna
  to the Son of David,' they were indignant. 'Do
  you hear what these children are saying?' they
  asked him. 'Yes,' replied Jesus, 'have you never
  read, From the lips of children and infants you
  have ordained praise?'" (Matthew 21:12-16 NIV)

PRAY TO BECOME A HOUSE OF PRAYER THAT IS
PLEASING TO GOD:

Dear God, I thank You that my body is a temple of the
Holy Spirit, who is in me, whom I have received from You (1
Corinthians 6:19). My desire is to be a House of Prayer according
to Your purpose for me. Please continually drive out anything
in me that is impure. Wash me thoroughly from my iniquity and
cleanse me from my sin. "Create in me a pure heart, O God, and
renew a steadfast spirit within me" (Psalm 51:2, 10 ESV). Please
heal me of my spiritual and physical infirmities_____
_____(Now, describe each one in specific detail)_____

_____.

Help me to be diligent to pray for others, asking You to heal
them of their physical and spiritual illnesses (James 5:16).

8

PAUSE IN PRAYER TO THINK ABOUT THOSE WHO
ARE PHYSICALLY OR SPIRITUALLY ILL.

WRITE THEIR NAMES HERE AS A REMINDER, AND/
OR REFER TO YOUR PRAYER NOTEBOOK.

PRAY FOR THE HEALING OF EACH PERSON ON THE LIST, GIVING TIME AND ATTENTION TO EACH ONE INDIVIDUALLY.

Great Physician, I bring to You _____ (Name of person who needs physical or spiritual healing)_____ who is _____ (Describe the problem)_____ . Please heal _____ (Name)_____ . Please strengthen (him/her) through this time of suffering. May Your will be done in Your timing and according to Your plan in (his/her) life.

PRAISE GOD IN PRAYER:

Almighty God, I praise You because You continually cleanse us from sin as You have promised (1 John 1:9). I praise You because You hear our prayers through Your Spirit who lives within those of us who are in Christ (1 Corinthians 6:19). My desire is to always be Your House of Praise. Always! "I love the house where You live, O Lord" (Psalm 26:8 NIV)! All praise and honor and glory belong to You, my wonderful God!

My RSVP 3

PAUSE. TAKE A DEEP BREATH OR TWO.

REFOCUS ON BEING IN GOD'S PRESENCE.

ENCOURAGE MYSELF WITH GOD'S PROMISE:

> "The Lord <u>MY</u> God is with <u>ME</u>.
> He is mighty to save.
> He will take great delight in <u>ME</u>,
> He will quiet <u>ME</u> with his love,
> He will rejoice over <u>ME</u> with singing."
> (Zephaniah 3:17 NIV personalized)

CONTINUE PRAYING:

Dear Heavenly Father, I know You are here with me and that You are delighted that I am spending time with You. Continue to quiet me so I can think and respond to Your words. Now, as I continue my prayer, I am asking the same thing the followers of Jesus asked so long ago, "Lord, teach us to pray" (Luke 11:1). Teach *me* to pray. Like Jesus I want to look toward heaven and know with certainty that You, my only source of eternal life (John 17:3), will hear and respond to my prayers. Increase my faith (Luke 17:5).

MEDITATE UPON THESE INSPIRED WORDS UNTIL
I AM CERTAIN I TRULY BELIEVE GOD HAS MADE
EVERYTHING AVAILABLE FOR *ME*—EVERYTHING I
NEED FOR LIVING ACCORDING TO HIS WILL:

"His divine power has given me everything I need
for life and godliness
through my knowledge of Him
who called me by His own glory and goodness."
(2 Peter 1:3 NIV paraphrased)

PRAY FOR DILIGENCE TO INCREASE MY
KNOWLEDGE OF HIM.

Father, thank You for Your inspired words. Thank You for
my Bible and the freedom I enjoy to read and understand what
I need for life and godliness. Thank You for calling me by Your
divine power, Your glory and Your goodness. My desire is to be
faithful to read and know the goodness of Your words so that
my life will be all You would have it to be.

Today, I renew my commitment to spend more time reading
Your Word. I promise to be diligent to make more opportunities
to come near to You with a sincere heart in faith (Hebrews 10:22).
I want to know You, God. I want to know all I can know about
You, even though I realize that my knowledge will not be
complete until I shall see You face to face (1 Corinthians 13:12).
But, everything I can know now, I want to know!

Loving Father, each day, as I lay my requests before You
and wait in expectation (Psalm 5:3), I believe that You will surely
listen (Psalm 66:17-19).

READ THROUGH THE PRAYER JESUS TAUGHT HIS
FOLLOWERS.

Our Father in heaven,

Hallowed by your name,

Your kingdom come,

Your will be done

On earth as it is in heaven.

Give us today our daily bread.

Forgive us our sins

As we also forgive everyone

Who sins against us.

And lead us not into temptation,

But deliver us from the evil one

For yours is the kingdom

And the power and the glory forever.

Amen.

Matthew 6:9-13 NIV and Luke 11:2-4 NIV blended

My RSVP 4

PRAY: "OUR FATHER IN HEAVEN"
(Matthew 6:9)

READ AND REFLECT ON THE PRIVILEGE OF
JOINING WITH JESUS AND HIS FOLLOWERS TO
PRAY *"Our"*.

> "Jesus, who makes people holy, and those who
> are made holy are from the same family. So he
> is not ashamed to call them his brothers and
> sisters." (Hebrews 2:11 NCV)

> Jesus said, "... whoever does the will of my
> Father in heaven is my brother and sister...."
> (Matthew 12:50 ESV)

PRAY A PRAYER OF THANKFULNESS:

Our Father, what a wonderful privilege it is to be made holy
through Jesus. I am humbled in the knowledge that as I repent
and confess my sins to You, You restore me and make me holy
in Your sight. Thank You for the blessing to be in the same
eternal family with Jesus so that together we may address You
as 'Our Father.' I am deeply thankful that Jesus is my brother
and that He is not ashamed of me.

MEDITATE UPON THE WORD: *"Father"*.

> "How great is the love the Father has lavished
> on us, that we should be called children of God!
> And that is what we are!" (1 John 3:1 NIV)

CONTINUE IN PRAYER:

Thank you, Our Father, for loving me and for calling me one of Your children! Help me to treasure the truth and reality of this fact. Strengthen me in my desire to be a faithful and loving child. May Your Spirit within me always cry, "Abba Father," and testify with my spirit that I am one of Your children (Romans 8:15-16).

There are times when my mind and mouth cannot seem to form the words and thoughts I desire to express to You in prayer. So many problems and concerns are on my heart. But, I believe and trust that the Spirit helps me in my weakness. When I do not know how to express myself adequately, I trust that the Spirit Himself intercedes for me with groans that words cannot express. As You search me, may my mind and will be in harmony with the mind of the Spirit. I know that in all things You work for the good of those who love You (Romans 8:26-28). You, *Father,* are working for my good! Thank You!

WRITE A FEW WORDS HERE ABOUT WHAT SEEMS 'IMPOSSIBLE' RIGHT NOW:

_____
_____
_____
_____
_____
_____
_____
_____
_____
_____
_____
_____
_____
_____

CONTINUE IN PRAYER:

Our Father, thank You for the example of Jesus and for His words that I now pray from my own heart: "Abba, Father, everything is possible for you" (Mark 14:36 NIV). Please hear my prayer about the things in my life that seem impossible to me. I release the "impossible" to You, *Father,* because I truly believe that everything is possible for You.

Our Father, I am anxious about _____
_____(Describe what seems 'impossible')_____
_____
_____

I know You do not want me to be anxious about anything, so I am coming to You in prayer and petition, with thanksgiving, trusting You to help in this situation where I am so helpless. I remember other times when the solution to my concerns seemed 'impossible' and hopeless, but You answered my prayers. Thank You for _____

_____ (Describe when God turned the _____

_____ 'impossible' into 'possible') _____

_____.

Please give me Your peace, which is outside the realm of my human understanding. May Your peace protect my heart and mind in Christ Jesus (Philippians 4:6-7).

PAUSE . . . WAIT FOR HIS PEACE TO CALM ME.

MEDITATE UPON THE WORDS: *"in Heaven"*

> "You have come to thousands upon thousands of angels in joyful assembly.... You have come to God... to Jesus the mediator !" (Hebrews 12:22-24a NIV selected)

VISUALIZE THE HEAVENLY REALM.

BE STILL . . . PAUSE . . . AND TRUST THAT I AM IN THE PRESENCE OF GOD.

My RSVP 5

HEAR THE ANGELS SAYING:

> "Holy, holy, holy is the Lord Almighty;
> The whole earth is full of his glory."
> (Isaiah 6:3 NIV)

PRAY: "HALLOWED BE YOUR NAME"
(Matthew 6:9)

Our Father in heaven, my heart rejoices in Your presence. I desire to bring You glory and honor in all that I say and do (Psalm 105:3). Please help me not to misuse Your name (Exodus 20:7). For the times I have done so, please forgive me and accept my repentance. I confess that in today's world where those all around use Your name with disrespect and profanity that it is sometimes difficult to guard my own words in moments when I speak before I think. Please know that I want to keep Your name holy. When I speak Your name, God, and the name of Jesus, my desire is that I will speak only with honor and respect!

May the words of my mouth and the meditation of my heart continue to be acceptable to You, *Holy Father.*

Accept my words of praise now, words that were first spoken in prayer by Your prophet Daniel:

"Blessed be <u>YOUR</u> name, God, for ever and ever;
wisdom and power are <u>YOURS</u>.
<u>YOU</u> change times and seasons.
<u>YOU</u> set up kings and depose them.
<u>YOU</u> give wisdom to the wise
and knowledge to the discerning.
<u>YOU</u> reveal deep and hidden things;
<u>YOU</u> know what lies in darkness, and
the light of <u>JESUS</u> dwells with <u>YOU</u>"
(Daniel 2:20-23 ESV paraphrased)

PRAISE WITH THE WORDS OF JESUS:

"I praise you, O Father,
Lord of heaven and earth."
(Luke 10:21 NASB)

MEDITATE ON JESUS:

"… the Father has sent his Son to be the Savior of the world. If anyone acknowledges that Jesus is the Son of God, God lives in him and he in God." (1 John 4:14-15 ESV)

"... God exalted him to the highest place and gave him the name that is above every name, that at the name of Jesus every knee should bow, in heaven and on earth and under the earth, and every tongue confess that Jesus Christ is Lord, to the glory of God the Father." (Philippians 2:9-11 NIV)

PRAY, CONFESS AND REAFFIRM:

- I BELIEVE Jesus is the Christ, the Son of God!
- I BELIEVE Jesus is the Savior of the world!
- I BELIEVE Jesus is *my* Savior and *my* Lord!

MEDITATE UPON THE NAMES OF THE HOLY SPIRIT:

- Wisdom (Isaiah 11:2)
- Understanding (Isaiah 11:2)
- Counsel (Isaiah 11:2)
- Power (Isaiah 11:2)
- Knowledge (Isaiah 11:2)
- Fear of the Lord (Isaiah 11:2)
- Truth (John 14:16)

PRAY:

Our Father, as I continue to beseech You in prayer, please keep my mind in harmony with the mind of Your Spirit. Please mold my wisdom and understanding to become more and more like Yours, and less and less like the world's. May Your words which are spirit and life (John 6:63) be my constant counsel. Please give me Your power to remain faithful to You. Help me to become more diligent to read Your word so that I might gain knowledge for living in this world. Please increase my awareness of Your judgment so that I might have a heart and mind that respect all You have said. My desire is to keep in step with the Spirit and to walk in Your truth.

ENCOURAGE MYSELF WITH THESE WORDS OF BLESSING:

> The grace of <u>MY</u> Lord Jesus Christ
> and the love of <u>MY</u> Heavenly Father
> and the fellowship of the Holy Spirit is <u>WITH ME</u> !
> (2 Corinthians 13:14 ESV personalized)

CONTINUE TO PRAY:

Heavenly Father, please help me to continually offer to You a sacrifice of praise—the fruit of lips that confess Your name (Hebrews 13:15). Help me not to focus so much on myself and my own problems and needs that I neglect to express to You just how important You are to me. I desire to tell You more often how much I love You and appreciate all that You do for me each day.

FROM THE FOLLOWING LIST OF 'Names of God' CHOOSE A NAME THAT MEETS YOUR NEED(S) AND THE DESIRE(S) OF YOUR HEART.

IN PRAYER ADDRESS THE FATHER BY THAT NAME AND THANK HIM FOR THE BLESSING GIVEN BECAUSE OF HIS NAME.

Example: When I am lonely

Dear Father whose name is "IAM the Lord Who is Always There" (Psalm 23:4; Matthew 28:20), today I feel so alone and I'm coming to You because with You I am never truly alone. You are my Friend (Isaiah 41:8; John 15:14-1). Your name IAM (Exodus 3:14) is my reminder that You always have been with me, You are with me now, and You will always be with me in the future and into eternity. I am so grateful for this and I thank You.

Example: When I am worried about my finances

Dear Father, I come to You right now because Your name is "IAM Provider" (Genesis 22:14). You have told me that if I will seek You first, all my needs will be met. I am trying not to worry about how I will live or what I will eat or wear (Matthew 6:25-33; Philippians 4:19). I am seeking You first so that I might claim Your promise. I am thanking You in advance for helping me with my financial problems because I trust Your promise to provide for me. Please increase my trust.

Example: When I am ashamed of myself

Dear Father, thank You so much that Your Son is my High Priest (Hebrews 2:17; 3:1; 4:14-15) and He speaks to You on my behalf when I have no excuse for my sinful words or behavior. Jesus knows my heart. He knows that I am ashamed. I come to You repenting and confessing my sin.

My appreciation overflows because Your Son is my Savior (Psalm 88:1; Matthew 1:21; Luke 2:1). Thank You for always being the Guardian of my Soul (Job 10:12, 14; Romans 8:31-39; 1 Peter 2:25).

WRITE THE DATE, NAME OF GOD, AND WHY I CALLED UPON THE PROMISE OF THIS SPECIFIC NAME. REMEMBER AND THANK HIM AGAIN.

_____
_____
_____
_____
_____
_____
_____
_____
_____
_____
_____
_____
_____
_____
_____
_____
_____
_____
_____
_____
_____
_____
_____

PRAY:

I PRAISE YOU BECAUSE YOUR NAME IS ...

- ❏ Almighty God (Genesis 17:1; Isaiah 54:5; Jeremiah 31:35; 2 Corinthians 6:17,18; Revelation 1:8)
- ❏ Advocate (Job 16:19-21; 1 Timothy 2:5; Hebrews 7:25 & 9:24)
- ❏ Bread of life (Exodus 25:30; Deuteronomy 8:3; Psalm 23:5; John 6:35)
- ❏ Creator (Genesis 1:1, 26; Colossians 1:15-16)
- ❏ Emmanuel (Isaiah 7:14; Matthew 1:22-23)
- ❏ Eternal God (Genesis 21:33; Exodus 15:18; 1 John 5:20)
- ❏ Everlasting Father (Isaiah 9:6; John 3:16; John 6:44-47)
- ❏ Friend (Isaiah 41:8; John 15:14-15)
- ❏ God of Comfort (Jeremiah 8:18; Romans 15:5; 2 Corinthians 1:3-7)
- ❏ God of the House of God (Genesis 35:7; Ephesians 1:22-23; Colossians 1:18)
- ❏ God of My Life (Psalm 42:8; Acts 17:28)
- ❏ Guardian of my Soul (Job 10:12,14; Romans 8:31-39; 1 Peter 2:25)
- ❏ Helper (Psalm 118:7; Hebrews 13:6)
- ❏ High Priest (Hebrews 2:17; 3:1; 4:14-15)
- ❏ Hope (Psalm 71:5; Matthew 12:21; Romans 15:13)
- ❏ Husband (Isaiah 54:5; Revelation 21:2,9)
- ❏ IAM THAT IAM (Genesis 2:4; Exodus 3:14; John 8:58-59; Hebrews 13:8; Revelation 1:8)
- ❏ IAM Healer (Exodus 15:26; Psalm 23:3; Psalm 147:3; 1 Peter 2:24)
- ❏ IAM Judge (Judges 11:27; John 8:50)

- ❑ I AM Life and Truth (Psalm 31:1; John 16:13)
- ❑ I AM Light (Psalm 27:1; John 8:12)
- ❑ I AM the LORD Who is All Powerful (Psalm 147:5;)
- ❑ I AM the LORD Who is Always There (Matthew 28:20; 2 Corinthians 6:16, Romans 8:39)
- ❑ I AM the LORD Who Makes You Holy (Exodus 31:13; Leviticus 20:7,8; Psalm 23:5; John 17:17; 1 Corinthians 1:2; Jude 24)
- ❑ I AM the LORD Who Sees You (Genesis 16:13; Psalm 33:13-14; John 4:29 and 6:64; Hebrews 4:13)
- ❑ I AM Peace (Judges 6:24; Isaiah 9:6; Psalm 23:2, John 14:27; Romans 5:1; Philippians 4:6-7; Colossians 3:15; 2 Thessalonians 3:16)
- ❑ I AM Provider (Genesis 22:14; Matthew 6:31-33; Philippians 4:19)
- ❑ I AM Your Refuge (Jeremiah 16:9-21; Psalm 91:9; John 17:11)
- ❑ I AM Righteousness (Jeremiah 23:5,6; 1 Corinthians 1:30)
- ❑ I AM the Rock (Genesis 49:24; Psalm 18:2; 1 Corinthians 10:4)
- ❑ I AM Shepherd (Psalm 23:1, Isaiah 40:11,John 10:14ff; 1 Peter 2:25)
- ❑ I AM Your Victory Banner (Exodus 17:15; Psalm 23:4; 1 Corinthians 15:57;2 Corinthians 2:14; 1 John 5:4-5,)
- ❑ King Most High (Psalm 47:2; John 1:49 and 18:33-37; 1 Timothy 6:15)
- ❑ Lamb of God (John 1:29; Revelation 13:8)
- ❑ Love (Psalm 59:17; 1 John 4:8,16)
- ❑ Savior (Psalm 88:1; Matthew 1:21, Luke 2:11; John 2:42)

My RSVP 6

PRAY: "YOUR KINGDOM COME"
(Matthew 6:10a)

VISUALIZE THE KING OF HEAVEN AND EARTH:

"Jesus' appearance was transformed so that his face shone like the sun, and his clothes became as white as light." (Matthew 17:2 NLT)

"I saw the Lord, high and exalted, seated on a throne; and the train of his robe filled the temple." (Isaiah 6:1 NIV)

"On his robe and on his thigh he has a name written, King of kings and Lord of lords." (Revelation 19:16 ESV)

"God reigns over the nations; God is seated on his holy throne." (Psalm 47:8 NIV)

THINK ABOUT WHERE THE KINGDOM IS:

"People will not say, 'Look, here it is!' or, 'There it is!' because God's kingdom is within you." (Luke 17:21 NCV)

PRAY ABOUT MY KING:

Almighty Father, accept my words of praise for Jesus, Who is truly the King of glory (Psalm 24:9). He is my King eternal, immortal, invisible, the only God. May He receive all my honor and glory forever and ever (1 Timothy 1:17). Help me to keep Jesus on the throne of my heart and in the forefront of my mind. May I always honor Him above all else. My desire is to always seek first the kingdom of God and His righteousness (Matthew 6:33 ESV).

EXAMINE MYSELF ...

> "... to see whether I am in the faith. Test myself.
> Do I not realize this about myself,
> that Christ Jesus is in me...
> unless... I fail the test."
> (2 Corinthians 13:5 ESV personalized)

TAKE THE TEST:

Yes / No   Am I in the faith ?

> "Now faith is the assurance of things hoped for, the conviction of things not seen." (Hebrews 11:1 ESV)

> "... for we walk by faith, not by sight."
> (2 Corinthians 5:7 ESV)

Is my faith sure of what I hope for [eternity] and certain of what I do not see [the heavenly kingdom, God the Father, His Son

Christ Jesus, and the Holy Spirit who testifies to everything through the words of Christ]? (Hebrews 11:1)

Yes / No   Is Christ Jesus in me ?

> "I have been crucified with Christ. It is no longer I who live, but Christ who lives in me. And the life I now live in the flesh I live by faith in the Son of God, who loved me and gave himself for me." (Galatians 2:20 ESV)

Yes / No   By faith, am I in Christ Jesus ?

> "For the wages of sin is death, but the gift of God is eternal life in Christ Jesus our Lord." (Romans 6:23 NKJV)

> "Repent and be baptized every one of you in the name of Jesus Christ for the forgiveness of your sins and you will receive the gift of the Holy Spirit. For the promise is for you and your children and for all who are far off, everyone the Lord our God calls to himself." (Acts 2:38-39 ESV)

> "And you also were included in Christ when you heard the message of truth, the gospel of your salvation. When you believed, you were marked in him with a seal, the promised Holy Spirit, who is a deposit guaranteeing our inheritance ...." (Ephesians 1:13-14 NIV)

"Through faith in Christ Jesus ... all of you who were baptized into Christ have clothed yourselves with Christ." (Galatians 3:26-27 NASB)

"... if you confess with your mouth, 'Jesus is Lord,' and believe in your heart that God raised him from the dead, you will be saved." (Romans 10:8-9 ESV)

"And the Lord added to their number day by day those who were being saved." (Acts 2:47 ESV)

Through faith I was baptized into Christ on

(Date) _____

"… he who is joined to the Lord
becomes one spirit with him."
(1 Corinthians 6:17 ESV)

Jesus said, "In that day you will know that
I am in my Father,
and you in me, and I in you."
(John 14:20 ESV)

Yes / No   **Am I holding firmly?**

"For we have come to share in Christ
if we hold our original conviction firmly to the very end."
(Hebrews 3:14 NIV)

CONTINUE MY PRAYER:

Our Father in heaven, I promise to examine myself often to be certain that I am in the faith, holding firmly, and seeking Your kingdom first in every aspect of my life. Thank You for placing Your spirit within me. I praise You because Jesus is faithful and true. He is the Word of God who has communicated to me everything I need for my life so that I know how to live to please You (2 Peter 1:3). Jesus is the King of Kings! He is the Lord of Lords! (Revelation 19:11-16) Jesus is the King of *my* life! He is *my* Lord!

MEDITATE ON KING JESUS, MY BRIDEGROOM:

"As the bridegroom rejoices over the bride, so shall your God rejoice over you." (Isaiah 62:5 ESV)

"To the church ... I promised you to one husband to Christ." (2 Corinthians 1:1, 11:2 NIV)

"He who is joined to the Lord is one spirit with him." (1 Corinthians 6:17 ESV)

CONTINUE PRAYING:

Our Father, and I address You as 'Our Father' because I come to You together with Jesus who is my friend, my Savior, my King, and my bridegroom. We share a one spirit relationship (1 Corinthians 6:17). I am humbled to have this eternal honor. The fact that You are rejoicing over me (Isaiah 62:5) further humbles me while giving me great joy in Your presence. Please help me to be faithful in this relationship so that when the day comes for me to see You face to face, Christ will be able to present me as part of His radiant church, without stain or wrinkle or any other blemish, but holy and blameless, forgiven and made holy by the washing of water through your word (Ephesians 5:25-27, 30). I remember the day I was baptized into Christ and I rejoice in the assurance that you clothed me in Christ Himself (Galatians 3:27).

HEAR THE INVITATION:

> "Hallelujah! For the Lord our God, the Almighty, reigns. Let us rejoice and be glad and give the glory to Him, for the marriage of the Lamb has come and His bride has made herself ready." (Revelation 19:6b-7 NASB)

> "The Spirit and the bride say, 'Come.' And let the one who hears say, 'Come.' And let the one who is thirsty come; let the one who wishes take the water of life without cost." (Revelation 22:16-18 NASB)

PRAY:

Thank You, *Father,* for Your invitation to attend the wedding supper of Jesus. I rejoice and am glad. I give You glory because of my invitation. I accept Your invitation with pleasure. As I await that day, please help me to do righteous acts for You so that I am always ready, dressed in fine linen, bright and clean, which You have given me to wear (Revelation 19:8). Your words are true. They are the hope of my life!

READ THESE ADAPTED WEDDING VOWS:

Will you have the bridegroom Jesus, King of kings,
to be your wedded husband,
to live together according to God's plan,
in holy marriage?
Will you serve Him, love, honor, and keep Him
in sickness and in health;
and forsaking all others
keep yourself only for Him,
so long as you both shall live (eternally!)?"

RESPOND IN PRAYER:

Dear God, You who rejoice over me as Your bride (Isaiah 62:5), I vow to live according to Your plan. I will serve You, love, honor, and keep You on the throne of my heart in sickness and in health. I promise to forsake all others and serve only You. I vow to be faithful to You for as long as I am upon this earth knowing that You have promised to take me into eternity so that we can live together forever.

ENCOURAGE MYSELF BY READING AND MAKING GOD'S PROMISES VERY PERSONAL:

"Who shall separate ME from the love of Christ?
Shall trouble or hardship or persecution
or famine or nakedness or danger or sword?

No, in all these things I am more than (a)conqueror
through him who loved ME.
For I am convinced that neither death nor life,
neither angels nor demons,
neither the present nor the future,
nor any powers, neither height nor depth,
nor anything else in all creation,
will be able to separate ME from the love of God
that is in Christ Jesus MY Lord."
(Romans 8:35, 37-39 NIV personalized)

"Therefore, what God has joined together,
let man not separate." (Matthew 19:6 NKJV)

PRAY WITH WORDS OF PRAISE:

Loving Father, thank You for Your assurance that nothing
will be able to separate me from Your love that is in Christ Jesus
my Lord and King, my eternal bridegroom. I trust You with all
my being to keep Your promise!

I PRAISE YOU, FATHER, AND THANK YOU BECAUSE . . .
(List a few of my blessings)

_____

_____

_____

_____

_____

_____

_____

_____

My RSVP 7

PRAY: "YOUR WILL BE DONE ON EARTH
AS IT IS IN HEAVEN"
(Matthew 6:10a)

Our Father in heaven, it is the desire of my heart that
You teach me to do Your will, for You are my God (Psalm 143:10).
Right now, in this moment, I reaffirm to You that my desire is
to join with the angels in heaven to do Your will.

I promise ...

> ... to allow You to rule in my life because
> Your kingdom is within me
> (Psalm 103:19, Luke 17:21)
> ... to praise You (Psalm 103:20)
> ... to do Your bidding (Psalm 103:20)
> ... to obey Your word (Psalm 103:20)
> ... to be Your servant and do Your will
> (Psalm 103:21)
> ... to worship You and Your Son Jesus
> (Hebrews 1:6)
> ... to come together with the family of God in
> joyful assembly (Hebrews 12:22)
> ... to look carefully into the plan of salvation
> (1 Peter 1:12)
> ... to be always in submission to You
> (1 Peter 3:21-22)

Please help me to live in accordance with Your Spirit and to have my mind set on what Your Spirit desires (Romans 8:5).

READ AND THINK ABOUT THE FOLLOWING:

"For this is the will of my Father, that everyone who looks on the Son and believes in him should have eternal life…." (John 6:40 ESV)

"…it is not the will of your Father who is in heaven that one of these little ones should perish." (Matthew 18:14 NKJV)

"I tell you, there is rejoicing in the presence of the angels of God over one sinner who repents." (Luke 15:10 NIV)

"Jesus answered, 'If people love me, they will obey my teaching. My Father will love them, and we will come to them and make our home with them.'" (John 14:23 NCV)

"Go out quickly into the streets and alleys of the town and bring in the poor, the crippled, the blind and the lame…. Go out to the roads and country lanes and make them come in, so that my house will be full." (Luke 14:21, 23 NIV)

"The Spirit and the bride say, 'Come!' And let the one who hears say, 'Come!'" (Revelation 22:17 ESV)

PAUSE IN PRAYER TO LET THE NAMES AND FACES OF THOSE I KNOW WHO ARE NOT LIVING ACCORDING TO GOD'S WILL COME TO MIND.

PRAY BY NAME FOR EACH ONE.

Abba, Father, my heart aches when I think of the people I know who are not living according to Your will. As I've read Your inspired instructions in the Scriptures, I have heard Your Spirit say, "Come!'" I know that Your church down through the ages has invited people to come to You. Help me also to extend Your invitation. I want so much for _____(Insert name)_____ to hear and accept your invitation to "Come" (Revelation 22:17).

Wonderfully Patient God, I know it is not Your will that _____ be lost (Matthew 18:14). Please help me not to look only to my own interests, but also to the interests of _____. May my attitude be the same as that of Christ Jesus who took the very nature of a servant (Philippians 2:4-5, 7). If there is anything I can say or anything I can do to help _____ to know about Your invitation to accept the love and eternal life You offer, please give me the right words and the right opportunity. Forgive me when I have become discouraged and disappointed so that I have grown weary in prayer. When I think it is impossible, sometimes I fail to remember that with You, *Father,* all things are possible. Increase my resolve so that I will not give up. Deepen my trust that You are doing everything possible so that _____ might be added to Your eternal family of believers (Galatians 6:9-10).

My RSVP 8

PRAY: "GIVE US TODAY OUR DAILY BREAD"
(Matthew 6:11)

Generous Father, for the food on my table and in my cupboards, I thank You. I can never thank You enough or too often for the many blessings You bring to me. May I always remember and be encouraged by Your promise to supply all my needs according to Your glorious riches in Christ (Philippians 4:19).

MEDITATE UPON GOD'S INSPIRED WORDS:

"Do not be anxious about anything,
but in everything by prayer and petition, with thanksgiving
present your requests to God."
(Philippians 4:6-7 NIV)

CONTINUE TO PRAY IN JESUS' NAME:

Tender-hearted Father, thank You for Your concern about my anxious thoughts. You understand my tendency to worry and fret about many things. Please increase my trust in You. Calm my anxious spirit and help me to be content in any and every situation (Philippians 4:12). Help me to come quickly to You with all my requests. Raise my awareness of my daily blessings so that I will develop a more thankful attitude in everything. Thank You for revealing through Your words that You want me to bring my requests to You.

And, *Father,* as I continue to pray about my needs, the thought comes to me that perhaps the reason I do not have what I need is because I have not asked You (James 4:2-3). Please forgive me for taking You for granted. Sometimes I think because You already know what I need, I don't need to ask. Help me to remember that prayer pleases You (Proverbs 15:8). Increase my desire to glorify You with thanksgiving because this is pleasing to You (Psalm 69:30-31).

EXAMINE THE MOTIVES FOR MY REQUESTS:

> "You ask and do not receive, because you ask with wrong motives, so that you may spend it on your pleasures." (James 4:3 NASB)

> "If our heart does not condemn us, we have confidence before God; and whatever we ask we receive from him, because we keep his commandments and do what pleases him...."
> (1 John 3:21-22 ESV)

CONTINUE IN PRAYER:

Dear Father, may the words of my mouth and the meditation of my heart continue to be acceptable to You. If You sense that my motives are not pure or not according to Your will, then be assured that I truly desire Your will to be done.

With thanksgiving in my heart I now make my personal, specific requests. *Father in heaven,* You have promised to give good gifts to those who ask You (Matthew 7:7-11). I'm asking . . .

(Make my specific requests here and now)

_____

_____

_____

_____

_____

_____

_____

_____

_____

_____

_____

_____

_____

_____

_____

_____

_____

_____

_____

_____

_____

_____

_____

_____

_____

_____

_____

_____

THINK ABOUT PEOPLE I KNOW WHO HAVE SPECIFIC
NEEDS. WRITE THEIR NAMES AND NEEDS HERE:

_____

_____

_____

_____

_____

_____

_____

_____

_____

_____

_____

_____

_____

_____

_____

_____

_____

_____

_____

_____

_____

_____

_____

_____

_____

PRAY FOR THEM AT THIS TIME.

Almighty God, Giver of everything, even though I can never give as abundantly as You give, may this fact never become an excuse to close my heart to the needs of others. I confess that there have been times when I did not want to share. Please keep my heart tender, compassionate and sensitive to the physical and spiritual needs of others. Help me to be the kind of cheerful giver that You love (2 Corinthians 9:11). May I give a good measure, pressed down, shaken together and running over (Luke 6:38). May I give a greater measure by doing for others as I would have them do for me if I were in similar circumstances (Matthew 7:12). Please always give me the ability to work and do something useful so that I will have something to share (Ephesians 4:28).

Now, *Father,* _____(Name of someone who has requested prayer)_____ is in my thoughts. (His/Her) specific need is _____(Describe the need and/or problem)_____. Please, *Father,* give what is asked according to Your will.

NOW, PRAY ABOUT SPIRITUAL BREAD.

Father, Provider of all my needs, give me today my spiritual bread. Thank You for Jesus, who declared (John 6:32-35), "I am the bread of life." Thank You for Your promise that if I will come to Him I will never go hungry. Forgive me for those times when I have spiritually starved myself. Hear the confession of my heart and know that I recommit myself to seeking spiritual nourishment in the reading of Your words.

O God, help me to be faithful to my desire to feed daily on every word that comes from Your mouth (Matthew 4:4). I truly believe that all scripture comes from You and is useful for me. Please teach me, rebuke me, correct me and train me in righteousness so that I may be thoroughly equipped for every good work (2 Timothy 3:16-17).

Bless Your words to the nourishment of my soul, *my Lord and Provider.*

My RSVP 9

PRAY: "FORGIVE US OUR SINS"
(Luke 11:4)

Our Father, I come to You now in the name of Jesus because Your name is "IAM the Lord Who Makes you Holy (Leviticus 20:7-8 NIV)." I cannot be holy without You. I desire to be blameless in Your sight so that at all times I will be ready for You to come. I don't know if You will come to me at my death, or if You will come to me on the last day when You come with Your angels and all the faithful who have gone to heaven ahead of me (1 Thessalonians 4:16-17). But, until we meet face to face, my desire is to be careful to lead a blameless life (Psalm 10:12). Sadly, the reality is: I am weak. At times I am careless, acting and speaking before I remember Your wise counsel and the example set for me by Jesus.

Truly, *Father,* please know that in spite of my weakness, my desire is to please You by living a holy and godly life as I look forward to Your soon coming (Revelation 22:20). Please strengthen my resolve to make every effort to be found spotless, blameless and at peace with You (2 Peter 3:10-11, 14).

PAUSE AND THINK ABOUT:

> "Those whom I love I rebuke and discipline.
> So be earnest, and repent. Here I am! I stand
> at the door and knock. If anyone hears my

voice and opens the door, I will come in and eat with that person, and they with me." (Revelation 3:19-20 NIV)

MY PRAYER CONTINUES:

Dear Father, thank You for loving me. Thank You for continually knocking at the door of my heart to draw my attention back to You. Thank You for not giving up on me. Thank You for loving me enough to rebuke and discipline me. I truly desire to repent each and every time that I sin against You. Please keep my heart tender. Do not let me become hardened and insensitive as if my actions and words do not really matter. Right now, I ask that You bring into my mind anything that I have done or said ... or failed to do or say ... that is not pleasing to You.

PAUSE IN PRAYER SO THAT AREAS IN MY LIFE WHICH ARE NOT PLEASING TO GOD CAN COME TO MIND.

IN PRAYER DESCRIBE MY SIN(S) CLEARLY AND SPECIFICALLY:

Father, I repent and confess to You that I _____
_____ (Describe my sins, one at a time) _____
_____.

Please forgive me. Please forgive my faults that are hidden even from my own understanding. Keep me also from willful sins; may they not rule over me. I desire to be blameless and innocent of great transgression (Psalm 19:12-13).

MEDITATE ON:

> "Christ loved us and gave himself up for us."
> (Ephesians 5:2 ESV)

CLOSE MY EYES.

- VISUALIZE JESUS ON THE CROSS.
- SEE MY SIN BEING PLACED UPON HIM.
- FEEL HIS LOVE FOR ME.
- WITH SPIRITUAL EARS, HEAR CHRIST SAY:

> "Father, forgive _____(my name)_____."

READ AND ACCEPT GOD'S PROMISES:

> "If I confess my sins, he is faithful and just to forgive my sins and cleanse me from all unrighteousness." (1 John 1:9 ESV paraphrased)

> "Blessed are they whose sins are forgiven, whose wrongs are pardoned. Blessed is the person whom the Lord does not consider guilty." (Romans 4:7-8 NCV)

CONTINUE MY PRAYER WITH THANKSGIVING.

Almighty Father, You are the great IAM—the only One who has made men and women holy in the past. You are the only One who can make me holy now, and the only One who will ever make me holy. I praise You for loving me! I thank You because You have forgiven me! Increase my faith in You so that I truly believe there is now no condemnation for the sins I have just confessed (Romans 8:1). Please help me to put out of my mind the guilt and shame that lingers. Help me to forget the past and let it go (Philippians 3:13-14). Help me to press on through each day of my life—today and into eternity. I resolve not to dwell on my past and to let You do a new thing in my life (Isaiah 43:18-19). Create in me a clean heart that will become more and more like Yours. I desire to be steadfast, dependable and faithful to You, *my Lord and Savior* (Psalm 51:10).

PAUSE AND THINK ABOUT ANYONE I MIGHT HAVE OFFENDED OR SINNED AGAINST. THEN PRAY:

Merciful Father, it is not easy for me to apologize. My pride and, perhaps, the fear of rejection make me want to avoid this responsibility. Help me. Give me resolve and strength of character to go to _____ (Name of person to whom I owe an apology) _____ because I _____ (Describe my sin against this person) _____

_____.

I hope my apology will be accepted and forgiveness given. Help me to settle matters quickly and try to be reconciled (Matthew 5:23-25). If it is too late to reverse the consequences of my actions and words, please help me to do what can be done so that we might continue our lives in an atmosphere of forgiveness and respect. Increase my love and respect for ____ (Name) ____. Help me to love _____ (Name) _____ as I love myself and as You love us both (Romans 13:7-10).

CONTINUE IN PRAYER PRAISING GOD:

To You, *Lord,* who are able to keep me from falling and to present me before Your glorious presence without fault and with great joy—to You my only God and my Savior be glory, majesty, power and authority, through Jesus Christ my Lord, before all ages, now and forevermore! Amen. (Jude 24-25 personalized)

My RSVP 10

PRAY: "FORGIVE US OUR SINS AS WE ALSO FORGIVE
EVERYONE WHO SINS AGAINST US"
(Luke 11:4)

CONTINUE PRAYING:

Our Father in heaven, You have been faithful to forgive
me and to cleanse me of all unrighteousness (1 John 1:9). I praise
and thank You because now my prayers can become powerful
and effective (James 5:16) as You have promised. Please help me
to imitate Jesus. Help me to live a life of love, just as Christ
loved me and gave Himself up for me (Ephesians 5:1-2). Increase
my resolve to walk as Jesus did (1 John 1:6). Help me always to
be ready in advance to forgive others just as through Jesus You
prepared my forgiveness long before I was born (Romans 5:8).

READ AND MEDITATE UPON GOD'S INSTRUCTIONS
AND WARNINGS:

> "For if you forgive other people when they sin
> against you, your heavenly Father will also
> forgive you. But if you do not forgive others
> their sins, your Father will not forgive your
> sins." (Matthew 6:14 NIV)

"Judge not, and you will not be judged. Condemn not, and you will not be condemned. Forgive, and you will be forgiven.... For with the measure you use, it will be measured back to you." (Luke 6:37-38 ESV)

"Get rid of all bitterness, rage and anger, brawling and slander, along with every form of malice. Be kind and compassionate to one another, forgiving each other, just as in Christ, God forgave you." (Ephesians 4:31-32 NIV)

"Be careful not to let the light in you become darkness." (Luke 11:35 NCV)

CONTINUE TO PRAY:

Father, I have read Your inspired warnings and instructions. I desire to do what You have said. Please increase my resolve to forgive those who have insulted, hurt, disappointed, wronged, abused, or spitefully used me. I know I must forgive, but I don't know if I can. I don't know if I really want to forgive. Help me to think about the consequences of my lack of forgiveness. Melt my heart, Lord!

THINK ABOUT THE CONSEQUENCES OF SAYING, "I CAN'T" OR "I WON'T FORGIVE":

"In anger his master <u>handed him over to the jailers to be tortured</u> ['by bitterness, rage, anger, brawling, slander, and every form of malice"

50

Ephesians 4:31-32 NIV]. This is how my heavenly Father will treat each of you unless you forgive your brother from the heart." (Matthew 18:21-35 NIV emphasis by author)

"I have forgiven in the sight of Christ... in order that Satan might not outwit us. For we are not unaware of his schemes." (2 Corinthians 2:10-11 NIV)

"Beloved, never avenge yourselves, but leave it to the wrath of God, for it is written, 'Vengeance is mine, I will repay,' says the Lord. To the contrary, if your enemy is hungry, feed him; if he is thirsty, give him something to drink; for by so doing you will heap burning coals on his head. Do not be overcome by evil, but overcome evil with good." (Romans 12:19-21 ESV)

PRAY WITH DETERMINATION:

O Lord, I do not want to be overcome by evil. I want to overcome evil with good. I vow from this time forward I will not let Satan outwit me because of my refusal to forgive (2 Corinthians 2:10-11). Vengeance is Yours (Romans 12:19). What was done to me is wrong, but I understand that forgiving does not mean that I'm saying everything is now alright. I understand forgiving means that I give up my desire for revenge and retribution. You are the Judge and You will punish in Your timing. As hard as it may be for me, I will look for ways to show Your loving kindness to those who sin against me. Even though it is very difficult at times to forgive, I praise You for

Your promise that I can do all things through Christ who gives me strength (Philippians 4:13).

NOW, PAUSE AND TEST MYSELF TO FIND OUT IF THERE ARE THOSE WHO COME TO MIND THAT I HAVE NOT FORGIVEN.

PRAY:

Heavenly Father, I forgive _____ (Name of the person who sinned against me)_____ for _____
_____ (Specific description of what was done or said) _____
_____.

Your kindness, *Father,* and that of Your Son has helped me toward repentance (Romans 2:4b). Please increase my ability to be kind to the one I have forgiven. If possible, may this kindness bring the desire to repent to ___ (Name) ___. My heart is prepared in advance to forgive face to face when an apology is given me, but until then, *Father,* in Your presence please know that I have forgiven ___ (Name) ___.

BE PREPARED FOR FUTURE SINS AGAINST ME:

> "'Lord, how often shall my brother sin against me, and I forgive him? Up to seven times?' Jesus answered, 'I tell you, not seven times, but seventy times seven.'" (Matthew 18:21-22 NKJV)

> "...forgive us our debts, as we forgive our debtors." (Matthew 6:12 NKJV)

"Give to everyone what you owe them (forgiveness).... Let no debt remain outstanding, except the continuing debt to love one another.... Love your neighbor as yourself. Love does no harm to a neighbor." (Romans 13:7-10 NIV)

PRAY:

Dear Lord, help me to prepare my mind and emotions for the future so that when wronged I will immediately turn to You. I promise to forgive as long as I need to be forgiven. You and I both know that as long as I live I will need forgiveness. May the joy of receiving Your forgiveness time and time again make it easier for me to forgive as many times as necessary.

Loving Father, increase my ability to treat those who sin against me as Jesus commanded. Help me...

> ... to love my enemies
> ... to do good to those who hate me
> ... to bless those who curse me
> ... to pray for those who mistreat me
> ... to be merciful, just as You Father are merciful
> ... not to judge
> ... not to condemn
> ... to forgive, and I will be forgiven
>> (Luke 6:27-37 personalized)

KEEP PRAYING:

And, *Father,* as I continue in prayer, please grant my desire to love in the way You love.

Give me firm resolve...

> ...to be patient and kind
> ...not to be rude
> ... not to be self-seeking
> ... not to be easily angered
> ... to keep no record of wrongs
> ... not to delight in evil (when something bad happens to the one who has sinned against me)
> ... to rejoice with the truth
> ... to protect
> ... to trust
> ... to hope
> ... to persevere
> ... to trust that 'Love never fails!'
> (1 Corinthians 13:4-8)

My RSVP 11

PRAY: "AND LEAD US NOT INTO TEMPTATION"
(Matthew 6:13a)

MEDITATE UPON JESUS, MY PERFECT EXAMPLE
WHEN FACED WITH TEMPTATION:

> "Then Jesus was led up by the Spirit into the
> wilderness to be tempted by the devil." (Matthew
> 4:1 ESV)

> "For we do not have a high priest [Jesus] who is
> unable to empathize with our weaknesses, but we
> have one who has been tempted in every way, just
> as we are—yet he did not sin." (Hebrews 4:15 NIV)

> "Since these children are people with physical
> bodies, Jesus himself became like them.... And
> now he can help those who are tempted, because
> he himself suffered and was tempted." (Hebrews
> 1:14, 18 NCV)

PRAY:

Our Father, it is with overwhelming gratitude that I thank
You for Jesus' example of suffering and strength that I can
focus upon when I am tempted. I confess that I do not always

struggle against temptation, and often give in too easily. Help me to grasp the reality that being like Jesus will require me to suffer when tempted if I want to be successful in my struggle against sin. Please share with me the same power that raised Jesus from the dead and the same power that He called upon to help overcome temptation. My gratitude overflows because Jesus was willing to share in my humanity so that He could help me when I am tempted.

READ AND THINK ABOUT GOD'S PROMISE:

> "If you think you are strong, you should be careful not to fall. The only temptation that has come to you is that which everyone has. But you can trust God, who will not permit you to be tempted more than you can stand. But when you are tempted, he will also give you a way to escape so that you will be able to stand it."
> (1 Corinthians 10:12-13 NCV)

CONTINUE TO PRAY FOR STRENGTH TO RESIST TEMPTATIONS:

Our Father, I believe that my temptations are common to all people. I also believe that You are faithful as You watch over my soul and that You will not let me be tempted beyond what I can bear. When I am tempted, please help me to find the way out which You promise to provide so that I will not sin. And, when I am under great pressure and think the temptation is beyond my ability to endure, may I not despair, thinking that I am alone and must resist in my own strength. Help me when tempted to rely on You and Your almighty power, and not on myself.

READ AND HOLD ONTO GOD'S WORDS:

> "He Himself [Jesus] has said, 'I will never desert
> you, nor will I ever forsake you." (Hebrews 13:5b
> NASB)

> "Remember, God is the One who makes you
> and us strong in Christ." (2 Corinthians 1:21 NCV)

PRAY:

Our Father, bring into my mind the truth that I am not alone. I want to remember always that You will never leave me and that You are the one who will make me stand strong when tempted. Please, do not let my heart be drawn to what is evil so that I take part in wicked deeds along with those who are evil doers (Psalm 141:4 NIV). You know that I have chosen the path of life (Psalm 16:11 NIV) that began when I took my first steps through the narrow gate that leads to eternal life (Matthew 7:13-14). If I have taken my eyes off the eternal goal, please forgive me and help me return to Your path of life.

PAUSE . . . . THINK ABOUT MY WEAKNESSES AND
MY TEMPTATIONS. THEN PRAY:

Almighty God, I am humbled in Your presence to put into words my weaknesses and temptations. You and I both know that I _____ (Describe my weaknesses) _____

_____

_____.

And, I am being tempted to _____
_____
_____.

Help me to be vigilant, to watch and pray so that I will not give in to temptation. My spirit is willing, but my body is weak (Mark 14:38).

Father, please give me Your strength and lead me away from temptation. I am willing to follow You out of harm's way. As You have promised, may I always be more than a conqueror (Romans 8:37).

Thank You that Jesus taught us to pray, "And lead us not into temptation." Help me always to pray and request that You protect me from wilderness experiences where I might be tempted to turn away from You. Protect me from myself and my worldly desires that would lure and entice me to sin against You (James 1:13-15). Please help me to choose my friends wisely and not to spend my time with evil companions (1 Corinthians 15:33). Help me to resist the devil and stand firm in my faith, trusting in Your power to deliver me (1 Peter 5:8-9). May I never fall in love with the world and its prideful riches and the desires of the flesh (1 John 1:15-17). May my eyes focus on You and the unseen realities that are eternal (2 Corinthians 4:18).

REAFFIRM IN PRAYER:

Our Father, my desire is that whatever I do, whether in word or deed, I will do all in the name of my Lord Jesus, giving thanks to You through Him (Colossians 3:17).

I reaffirm to you that the desire of my heart is . . .

- to honor You with my body
  (1 Corinthians 6:20)
- to flee from sexual immorality
  (1 Corinthians 6:18)
- to flee from the love of money
  (1 Timothy 6:10-11)
- to flee from evil desires
  (2 Timothy 2:22)
- to put to death whatever belongs to my earthly nature
  (Colossians 3:5)
- to put to death greed which is idolatry
  (Colossians 3:5)
- to rid myself of anger, rage, malice, slander, and filthy language (Colossians 3:8)
- not to lie (Colossians 3:8)
- to set my heart and mind on things above
  (Colossians 3:1-2)
- to pursue righteousness, faith, love and peace
  (2 Timothy 2:22)

REMEMBER OTHER PEOPLE:

> "The only temptation that has come to you is that which everyone has." (1 Corinthians 10:12 NCV)

> "...if anyone is caught in any transgression, you who are spiritual should restore him in a spirit of gentleness. Keep watch on yourself, lest you too be tempted." (Galatians 6:1 ESV)

"Refuse to give in to (the devil), by standing strong in your faith. You know that your Christian family all over the world is having the same kinds of suffering." (1 Peter 5:9 NCV)

PRAY FOR OTHERS WHO ARE BEING TEMPTED:

Our Father, please hear my prayer and come to the aid of _____(Name of person being tempted)_____ who is being tempted. Increase _____(Name)_____'s faith so (he/she) will trust You for wisdom and courage. And, may _____(Name)_____ resolve not to sin rather than give in. If there is anything I can do to help, please give me the opportunity to speak the words You would want me to speak. May what I say and do be done with Your spirit of gentleness and love. But, in my desire to comfort and help, do not let me be led into the same temptation. May I always remember that Jesus taught His followers to pray, "Lead *us* not into temptation." May we always pray for each other!

My RSVP 12

PRAY: "DELIVER US FROM THE EVIL ONE"
(Matthew 6:13b)

PAUSE AND VISUALIZE THE ENEMY:

> "And the great dragon was thrown down, that ancient serpent, who is called the devil and Satan, the deceiver of the whole world—he was thrown down to the earth, and his angels were thrown down with him." (Revelation 12:9 ESV)

> "For our struggle is not against flesh and blood, but against the rulers, against the authorities, against the powers of this dark world and against the spiritual forces of evil in the heavenly realms." (Ephesians 6:11-12 NIV)

> "Be sober-minded; be watchful. Your adversary the devil prowls around like a roaring lion, seeking someone to devour." (1 Peter 5:8 ESV)

CONTINUE IN PRAYER:

All-powerful God and Loving Father, I submit myself to You. As I continue to come near to You in prayer, I know You have come near to me just as You promised (James

4:7-8). Please deliver me from Satan, the evil one. My resolve and desire is to resist the devil, knowing that You have promised he will flee from me when I do so. Help me to be self-controlled and alert, resisting him and standing firm in my faith in You. It is a sad and terrible thing to see daily the devastation that the evil one has brought upon this earth. Your wisdom and protection are needed by everyone. Help me to fight for and hold onto my faith with full assurance that because I have been born of God I will overcome the world (1 John 5:4). I trust You and I praise You because You always lead Your followers in triumphal procession in Christ (2 Corinthians 2:14).

VISUALIZE DRESSING MYSELF FOR BATTLE:

> "...put on the armor of light. Let us walk properly as in the daytime, not in orgies and drunkenness, not in sexual immorality and sensuality, not in quarreling and jealousy. But put on the Lord Jesus Christ...." (Romans 13:12-14 ESV)

> "Therefore take up the whole armor of God, that you may be able to withstand in the evil day, and having done all, to stand firm... praying at all times in the Spirit...." (Ephesians 6:13, 19 ESV)

PRAY:

God and Father of all who desire to follow You into eternal life, You know from my promises and prayers that I am trying to put aside all deeds of darkness and put on the armor of light (Romans 13:12). Having been resurrected from the waters of baptism, You clothed me with Jesus Christ, my Lord and Savior (Romans 13:14). Daily, in prayer and the reading of Your word, I will put on Your full armor so that I can take my stand against the devil's schemes (Ephesians 6:11).

VISUALIZE PUTTING ON MY BELT OF TRUTH:

> "Stand therefore, having fastened on the belt of truth...." (Ephesians 6:14 ESV)

PRAY:

Father, I promise to hold to the teachings of Jesus so that I will know the truth (John 8:31-32). His eternal words of truth will be my protection against all false teachers and worldly philosophies.

VISUALIZE PUTTING ON MY BREASTPLATE:

> "...and having put on the breastplate of righteousness...." (Ephesians 6:14 ESV)

PRAY:

Praise to you, Father, because Jesus is my breastplate of righteousness. Thank You for His righteousness that replaces my own unrighteousness (2 Corinthians 5:21) so that I am protected because of faith and love (1 Thessalonians 5:8). Increase my faith. Increase my love.

VISUALIZE PUTTING ON MY SHOES:

> "…and, as shoes for your feet, having put on the readiness given by the gospel of peace." (Ephesians 6:15 ESV)

PRAY:

God, You are my Eternal Commander and the director of my steps! It is my desire to live by Your Spirit and to keep in step with Your Spirit (Galatians 5:25). I want to walk as Jesus did so that I will always be able to live and move and have my very existence in You (1 John 1:6; Acts 17:28). Help me to become more and more comfortable in my spiritual shoes. Lead me and help me, for the sake of the gospel, to always be prepared to give an answer to everyone who asks me to explain the faith and hope that I have in You (1 Peter 3:15). Help me to hear Your cadence sounding off reminding me to show greater love, joy, peace, patience, kindness, goodness, faithfulness, gentleness, and self-control (Galatians 5:22-23).

VISUALIZE TAKING UP MY SHIELD:

> "In all circumstances take up the shield of faith, with which you can extinguish all the flaming arrows of the evil one…." (Ephesians 6:16 NIV)

PRAY:

God Most High, Your faithfulness is my strength and my shield (Psalm 91:4, 7:10, 28:7). I will hold onto this knowledge by faith. I praise You for saving me. My heart trusts in You and I am helped (Psalm 7:10, 28:7). I will not fear the evil one and his attacks against me. May his flammable accusations, scorching temptations, or smoldering problems never burn away my faith and trust in You. When the evil one draws his bow, let the arrows fall short (Psalm 58:7). I am clinging to Your promise to rescue me from every evil attack and bring me safely into Your heavenly kingdom (2 Timothy 4:17-18). Even though I may walk through the valley of death, I will fear no evil because You are with me. You comfort me (Psalm 23:4) and I thank You for this wonderful blessing.

VISUALIZE PUTTING ON MY HELMET:

"...and take the helmet of salvation...." (Ephesians 6:17 ESV)

PRAY:

O Sovereign Lord, my strong deliverer, who shields my head in the day of battle, do not grant the wicked their desires and do not let their plans succeed (Psalm 140:7-8). Help me to be self-controlled, filling my thoughts with the hope of salvation as a helmet. Thank You for the salvation You are giving me through my Lord Jesus Christ (1 Thessalonians 5:8-9). As I struggle and fight through life's battles, sharing each one with You, please give me Your promised peace which transcends all understanding. Guard my heart—my emotions. Guard my mind—my thoughts and my will—in Christ Jesus (Philippians 4:7).

VISUALIZE TAKING UP MY SWORD:

> "…and (take) the sword of the Spirit which is the
> word of God…." (Ephesians 6:17 ESV)

PRAY:

Mighty God, my Wisdom and Power, prepare my
mind for action (1 Peter 1:13). Help me to take captive every
thought to make it obedient to Christ (2 Corinthians 10:3-5). Every
word of Yours is flawless (Proverbs 30:5). Your words that were
spoken through Jesus are spirit and they are life (John 6:3). Help
me to increase my skill with the sword of the Spirit. Give me the
skill I need to use Your words to be able to demolish arguments
and every falsehood that sets itself up against the knowledge of
God (2 Corinthians 10:3-5). I vow not only to hear Your words, but
to do them. I will hate evil and cling to what is good (Romans
12:9). I love You, *Father,* and I thank You for guarding my life
and delivering me from the hand of the wicked (Psalm 97:10).

REJOICE AND PRAISE GOD BECAUSE …

> "He has delivered us from such a deadly peril,
> and he will deliver us again.
> On him we have set our hope
> that he will continue to deliver us."
> (2 Corinthians 1:10 NIV emphasis by author)

66

WRITE NAMES OF PEOPLE I DESIRE TO BE
DELIVERED FROM THE EVIL ONE:

- My immediate family
- My church family
- My friends, neighbors and coworkers
- My city, my country, my government
- My brothers and sisters in the church throughout the world

_____   _____
_____   _____
_____   _____
_____   _____
_____   _____
_____   _____
_____   _____
_____   _____
_____   _____
_____   _____
_____   _____
_____   _____
_____   _____
_____   _____
_____   _____
_____   _____

NOW, PRAY THESE NAMES
INTO THE FOLLOWING PRAYER.

PRAY FOR OTHERS TO BE DELIVERED:

Our Father in heaven, I've asked You to deliver me and I'm trusting that You will deliver me again and again and again. I've set my hope upon the eternal fact that You will continue to deliver me.

Now, I want to change my focus from 'deliver *me*' to pray, asking You to deliver *us* from the evil one. I want to be very specific and ask You to deliver _____(Name)_____ from every evil influence and from every lie and deception that might undermine (his/her) relationship with You, and from every physical illness or disaster. But, if any of us do find ourselves in the midst of a disaster, may we never fear the one who can destroy our bodies—never fear because we know we have an eternal home with You (Luke 12:4-7). Please protect _____ and give (him/her) courage and wisdom to resist the evil one. May the arrows from the evil one fall short of their aim to hurt _____ (Psalm 58:7). Please rescue (him/her) from every evil attack and bring (him/her) safely into Your heavenly kingdom (2 Timothy 4:17-18).

My desire is the same as Yours, that none of these little ones perish (Matthew 18:14); and, we are all Your little ones. Even though the evil one may roar through sinful activity and temptation, physical and mental disease, and all kinds of natural disasters, please protect _____ from eternal death.

May each of us stay alert and watchful, firm in faith until the day we stand in the courts of heaven praising You. May those for whom we've prayed stand victorious because we have overcome by Your power!

My RSVP 13

PRAY: "FOR YOURS IS THE KINGDOM
AND THE POWER AND THE GLORY
FOREVER. AMEN."
(Matthew 6:13)

PRAY AND PRAISE GOD FOR HIS KINGDOM:

Eternal God and Our Father in heaven, You are my King and my Savior. Thank You for rescuing me from the dominion of darkness and bringing me into the kingdom of Your Son whom You love (Colossians 1:13). Thank You for Your promise to rescue me from every evil attack so that You might bring me safely into Your eternal, heavenly kingdom (2 Timothy 4:18).

It truly humbles me to know that You crown me with salvation (Psalm 149:4). May praises to You always be in my mouth. May You always take delight in me. I will always delight myself in You (Psalm 37:4). I give You thanks because You are good. Your love endures forever (Psalm 107:1-2). Help me to be joyful always and to give thanks in all circumstances. Increase my desire to pray continually (1 Thessalonians 5:16-18) so that I might always enjoy the pleasure of Your company.

I praise You, my God, my King—eternal, immortal, invisible. You are the only God and I promise to give You honor and glory for ever and ever (1 Timothy 1:17).

MEDITATE UPON THE POWER OF GOD AVAILABLE FOR ME:

> "He gives strength to those who are tired and more power to those who are weak.... The people who trust in the Lord will become strong again." (Isaiah 40:29-31 NCV)

> "By his power God raised the Lord from the dead, and he will raise us also." (1 Corinthians 6:14 NIV)

> "I can do all things through Christ who strengthens me." (Philippians 4:13 NKJV)

PRAY AND PRAISE GOD FOR HIS POWER:

Almighty and Powerful God, I thank You and praise You because You give me strength when I am weary, and You increase my power when I am weak. Please continually renew my hope as You strengthen me again and again day by day (Isaiah 40:29-31). You raised Jesus from the dead by Your power, and I trust You to raise me from death also (1 Corinthians 6:14). I will speak and sing of Your strength and Your love (Psalm 59:16). Because You have promised, I know that I can do everything because of the strength You give me through Christ (Philippians 4:13).

MEDITATE UPON GOD'S GLORY:

> "Here is the message we have heard from Christ and now announce to you: God is light, and in him there is no darkness at all." (1 John 1:5 NCV)

"The Son is the radiance of God's glory and the exact representation of his being...." (Hebrews 1:3 NIV)

"And we all, with unveiled face, beholding the glory of the Lord, are being transformed into the same image from one degree of glory to another. For this comes from the Lord who is the Spirit." (2 Corinthians 3:18 ESV)

"For God, who said, 'Light shall shine out of darkness,' is the One who has shone in our hearts to give the Light of the knowledge of the glory of God in the face of Christ." (2 Corinthians 4:6 NASB)

CONTINUE IN PRAYER, REQUESTING GOD TO HELP ME REFLECT HIS GLORY:

Glorious God in Heaven, You are the source of all light. In You there is no darkness at all (1 John 1:5). I truly believe and reaffirm that Jesus is the radiant glory and the exact representation of Your being (Hebrews 1:3). It is my desire to reflect Jesus with ever-increasing glory (2 Corinthians 3:18). Please mold me and make me into a person of integrity. Help me to pay no attention to those around me who might draw me away from You. Help me to do and to speak only that which is in accordance with Your truth (Mark 12:14). Forgive me for those times when my own opinions and personal philosophy of life were of greater importance than Your will. May I never again live or speak to gain honor for myself. May I live in such a way that You are honored. May there never again be anything false in me (John 7:16-18).

VISUALIZE GOD BRINGING ME INTO HIS GLORY:

"Now if we are children, then we are heirs—heirs of God and co-heirs with Christ, if indeed we share in his sufferings in order that we may also share in his glory. I consider that our present sufferings are not worth comparing with the glory that will be revealed in us." (Romans 8:17-18 NIV)

"And after you have suffered a little while, the God of all grace, who has called you to his eternal glory in Christ, will himself restore, confirm, strengthen, and establish you." (1 Peter 5:10 ESV)

READ AND ACCEPT GOD'S INVITATION:

"Come to me, all you who are weary and burdened, and I will give you rest. Take my yoke upon you and learn from me, for I am gentle and humble in heart, and you will find rest for your souls." (Matthew 11:28-29 NIV)

PRAY AND PRAISE GOD:

Loving Father and God of All Comfort, thank You so much for Your invitation to come to You to find rest for my soul. In the pleasure of Your company I am truly finding rest from the weariness of life. 'Thank You' does not adequately express my deep gratitude to Jesus who was made perfect through suffering (Hebrews 2:10) so that, through Him,

I might have the opportunity and blessing to come into Your presence. As difficult and painful as life's circumstances can be, I praise You for the privilege of sharing in Jesus' sufferings in order that I might also share in His glory (Romans 8:17-18). The disappointments, illnesses, injustices, and heartaches in my life are not worth comparing to the eternal glory that You have promised me in Christ. Help me to remember and draw strength from Your promise that after I have suffered a little while, You will restore me and make me strong, firm and steadfast (1 Peter 5:10).

Your throne, *King of kings and Lord of lords,* will last for ever and ever (Hebrews 1:8). May the whole earth be filled with Your glory (Psalm 57:19). To You, Father, as You sit on the throne and to Jesus, the Lamb, who sits at Your right hand, forever and ever I give You my praise and honor because of Your glory and power (Revelation 5:13). I am rejoicing in You because You are eternal, and in You I am sharing in Your eternity.

MEDITATE UPON 'IN JESUS NAME':

> Jesus said, "Truly, truly, I say to you, whatever you ask of the Father in my name, he will give it to you. Until now you have asked nothing in my name. Ask, and you will receive, that your joy may be full." (John 16:23-24 ESV)

> "Because Jesus lives forever... he is able to save completely those who come to God through him, because he always lives to intercede for them." (Hebrews 7:24-25 NIV)

PRAY AND THANK GOD IN THE NAME OF JESUS:

Eternal God, as I come to the close of my prayer, my gratitude continues to overflow because I know that Jesus is interceding for me (Hebrews 7:24-25). If I have prayed anything that is not according to Your will, please know my desire is for You to answer my prayer only in accordance with Your will. My joy is complete, knowing that I have made my requests in the name of Jesus. I anticipate that I will receive as You have promised (John 16:23-24).

READ AND MEDITATE UPON THE WORD 'AMEN':

"These are the words of the Amen, the faithful
and true witness, the ruler of God's creation."
(Revelation 3:14 NIV)

PRAY AND THANK GOD:

Our Father, my King, my Power, my Glory, thank You for Jesus whose very name is 'Amen'. My desire is to say 'Amen! So be it!' to everything You reveal to me through the words of Jesus. Thank You for inspiring men to share Your love and wisdom and plan of salvation in words so I can read and hear You speaking to me. I praise You for the truth in all Your words. Every word that Jesus spoke and every word written from Genesis through Revelation is true and I accept Your words as truth. As I speak, may I always do it as one speaking Your very words as the foundational truth of my life. When I serve, may I do it with the strength that You provide so that in all things You may be praised (1 Peter 4:11). Please keep me from falling so that now and into eternity I will always be welcomed into Your glorious presence without fault and with great joy (Jude 1:25). Help me to grow in the grace and knowledge of my Lord and Savior Jesus Christ (2 Peter 3:18).

And now, "May the words of my mouth and the meditation of my heart be pleasing in your sight, O LORD, my Rock and my Redeemer" (Psalm 19:14 NIV).

I pray in the name of Jesus, the Amen, the faithful and true witness, the ruler of God's creation (Revelation 3:14).

"Amen!
Praise and glory and wisdom and thanks
and honor and power and strength be
to you, our God and Father
for ever and ever.
Amen!"
(Revelation 7:12 NIV)

Hear With Spiritual Ears

HEAR MYSELF INCLUDED IN THESE PRAYERS.

Hear Jesus praying for me

"I pray also for those who will believe in me through their (the apostles') message, that all of them may be one, Father, just as you are in me and I am in you. May they also be in us so that the world may believe that you have sent me. I have given them the glory that you gave me, that they may be one as we are one: I in them and you in me. May they be brought to complete unity to let the world know that you sent me and have loved them even as you have loved me. Father, I want those you have given me to be with me where I am, and to see my glory, the glory you have given me because you loved me before the creation of the world!" (John 17:20-24 NIV)

Hear Paul praying for me

"For this reason I bow my knees before the Father, from whom every family in heaven and on earth is named, that according to the riches of his glory he may grant you to be strengthened with power through his Spirit in your inner being, so that Christ may dwell in your hearts through faith—that you, being rooted and grounded in love, may have strength to comprehend with all the saints what is the breadth and length and height and depth, and to know the love of Christ that surpasses knowledge, that you may be filled with all the fullness of God. Now to him who is able to do far more abundantly than all that we ask or think, according to the power at work within us, to him be glory in the church and in Christ Jesus throughout all generations, forever and ever. Amen." (Ephesians 3:14-21 ESV)

Hear Peter praying for me

"Grow in the grace and knowledge of our Lord and Savior Jesus Christ. To him be the glory both now and forever! Amen." (2 Peter 3:18 NKJV)

Hear Jude praying for me

"To him who is able to keep you from stumbling and to present you before his glorious presence without fault and with great joy—to the only God our Savior be glory, majesty, power and authority, through Jesus Christ our Lord, before all ages, now and forevermore! Amen." (Jude 1:24-25 NIV)

My
RSVP

Prayer Prompt Guide

Copy or remove
the front-and-back page outline that follows.
Keep it in your Bible or your Journal
as a quick reference and prayer prompter.

My RSVP
to accept God's invitation to enjoy
The Pleasure of His Company

Jesus said, When you pray say,

OUR FATHER IN HEAVEN
Pause. Be still. Think about each word. Meditate upon my eternal family - Jesus my brother (Heb 2:11), my brothers and sisters who are the children of our Father (Mat 12:50; 1 Jn 3:1). Thank God for His family. See myself coming hand in hand with Jesus to the throne of Our Father, surrounded by angels (Ps 73:23-25, Heb 12:22-24)

HALLOWED BE YOUR NAME
Reaffirm to God that I will not misuse His name, but will speak it only with honor and respect (Ex 20:7, Ps 105:3). Think about God's names and praise Him for meeting my needs because of the blessing promised in each name. Encourage myself because the grace of Jesus, the love of the Father, and the fellowship of the Holy Spirit are with me (2 Cor 13:14).

YOUR KINGDOM COME
Open my mind to let Jesus take His rightful place as King of everything in my life (Ps 24:9, 1 Tim 1:17). Examine myself to be certain that I am seeking first His kingdom and righteousness (2 Cor 13:5, Mat 6:33-34). Rearrange my priorities as needed.

Think about Jesus my bridegroom (Is 62:5; Eph 5:25-27,30; 2 Cor 1:1, 11:2; Rev 19:7-9). Encourage myself because nothing can separate me from Jesus (Rom 8:35-39, Mat 19:6).

YOUR WILL BE DONE ON EARTH AS IT IS IN HEAVEN
Pray: Teach me to do your will (Ps 143:10). Recommit to allow God to rule in my life (Ps 103:19, Lk 17:21), to praise, to do His bidding, to obey His word, to be his servant and do His will (Ps 103:21), to worship Jesus (Heb 1:6), to come together with the family of God in joyful assembly (Heb 12:22), to look carefully into the plan of salvation (1 Pet 1:12).

Pray for those who come to mind who are lost (Mat 18:14, 28:19-20; Lk 14:21,23; Jn 1:12-13). Pray for opportunities to be a servant of God's will (Phil 2:4,5,7; Gal 6:9-10).

GIVE US TODAY OUR DAILY BREAD
Present my requests to God (Phil 1:4-6, Jam 4:2-3). Meditate upon God's promises to meet my needs (Mat 7:7-11, Phil 4:19). Examine my motives for selfishness (Jam 4:3). Ask God to guide me in my obedience to give (Mat 7:11-12; Lk 6:38).

Thank God for His words—my spiritual bread (Mat 4:4; Jn 6:32-35, 2 Tim 3:16-17). Nourish myself by reading the Bible.

Pray for people who have asked me to pray about their needs.

AND FORGIVE US OUR SINS

Think about Jesus' coming again (1 Th 4:16-17; Rev 22:20). Am I ready? Ask the Holy Spirit to reveal areas in my life that are not pleasing to God so that I can confess them and be free from their effects (Ps 19:12-13, 2 P 3:10-11,14; Rev 3:19-20).

Visualize Jesus on the cross. See my sin placed on Him. Feel His love for me. With spiritual ears, hear Him say, "I forgive you!" (1 Jn 1:7-9) Apologize to anyone I have offended (Mat 5:23-25; Rom 13:7-10).

AS WE ALSO HAVE FORGIVEN THOSE WHO SINNED AGAINST US

Forgive others (Mat 6:14; Lk 6:37-38; Rom 13:7-10; Eph 4:31-32). Pray for repentance in the one who sinned against me (Rom 2:4b). Pray to be prepared for those who will sin against me in the future. Make up my mind to return good for evil (Mat 18:21-22; Rom 12:19-21). Pray for those who mistreat me (Lk 6:27-37; Mat 5:44). Ask God to increase my strength and resolve to love others (1 Cor 13:4-8).

LEAD US NOT INTO TEMPTATION

Watch for temptation from myself, my companions, and worldly desires (Jam 1:13-15; Gal 6:1; 1 Cor 15:33; 1 Jn 2:16-17). Claim God's promise not to let me be tempted beyond what I can bear (1 Cor 10:13). When tempted, pray for help finding God's promised way out (1 Cor 10:13). Remind myself that Jesus will help me (Heb 2:14,18; 4:15; 13:5b; 2 Cor 1:21).

Vow to honor God with my body (1 Cor 6:20), to flee from sexual immorality, greed, love of money, and evil desires (1 Cor 6:18, 10:14; Col 3:5; 1 Tim 6:6-10, 2 T 2:22). Vow to rid myself of anger, rage, malice, slander, filthy language, telling lies (Col 3:5-8).

BUT DELIVER US FROM THE EVIL ONE

Be self-controlled and alert for the devil's temptations (1 Pet 5:8-10). Resist the evil one (Jam 4:7-8). Put on God's armor of light (Rom 13:12,14, Eph 6:11-18) ...

> Belt of Truth (Jn 8:31-32, 14:6)
> Breastplate of Righteousness (2 Cor 5:21)
> Shoes of Readiness (Rom 10:15; Gal 5:25; 1 Jn 1:6)
> Shield of Faith (Heb 11:1,6, Ps 7:10, 28:7, 91:4)
> Helmet of Salvation (1 Th 5:8-9; Ps 140:7-8; Phil 4:7)
> Sword of the Spirit = Words of God (Eph 6:17-18; Jn 6:3; 1 Pet 1:13)

FOR YOURS IS THE KINGDOM,
AND THE POWER AND THE GLORY FOREVER

Praise God because He has invited me to be a participant with Him
> ... in His Kingdom (Col 1:13; 2 Tim 4:18; 1 Tim 1:17)
> ... in His Power (Isa 40:29-31; 1 Cor 6:14; Phil 4:13)
> ... in His Glory (Heb 1:3; 2 C 3:18, Heb 2:10; Rom 8:17-18; 1 Pet 5:10)

Meditate upon eternity (Heb 1:8, Ps 57:19; Rev 5:13)

IN JESUS NAME, AMEN.

Close my prayer in Jesus name, acknowledging Him as my intercessor (Jn 16:23-24; Heb 7:24-25). Say Jesus' name, "Amen." (Rev 3:14)

"PRAY CONTINUALLY,
give thanks in all circumstances,
for this is God's will for you in Christ Jesus."
1 Thessalonians 5:17-18 NIV

Also Available

To go with

My RSVP Prayer Guide

God invites you to enjoy
*The Pleasure
of His Company*

The Pleasure of His Company may be used for a quarterly group Bible study series. It may also be read by the one who desires a renewal of commitment in their own prayer life.

http://judywarpole.com

CPSIA information can be obtained at www.ICGtesting.com
Printed in the USA
LVOW07s1452051013

355510LV00001B/3/P